VOL.1 ISSUE 1 — GIRLY

PENELOPE GIRLY BE THE COVER GIRL!

THE HAUTE LIST 13
With so many things to keep track of, jot down the important stuff on the Haute List!

EVERY FASHIONISTA ... 24
Breaks the rules, stand out from the crowd and do your own thing.

YOU AS A COVER GIRL 42
Inquiring minds want to know the likes and thoughts of our cover girl! Find out here.

YOU WEAR IT WELL! 53
Timeless trends that never go out of style!

ARMED AND FABULOUS 77
Get armed with the top 10 tools that will keep you fabulous at all times!

PASSION FORWARD! 108
Passion Forward is a state of mind that many people aspire to be! Take a risk and follow your heart!

PENELOPE

VOL.I ISSUE I

GIRLY

PUBLISHED BY	KEE2CREATIVITY
ART AND DESIGN	ARKEELAUS D. SHERMAN

COPYRIGHT © 2011-2012
ALL RIGHTS RESERVED.
NO PART OF THIS BOOK MAY BE REPRODUCED, SCANNED OR DISTRIBUTED IN ANY PRINTED OR ELECTRONIC FORM WITHOUT PERMISSION. PLEASE DO NOT PARTICIPATE IN OR ENCOURAGE PIRACY OF COPYRIGHTED MATERIALS IN VIOLATION OF THE AUTHOR'S RIGHTS. PURCHASE ONLY AUTHORIZED EDITIONS.

ISBN: 978-0615525396

DEDICATIONS

THE PENELOPE GIRLY SERIES IS DEDICATED TO MY BIGGEST INSPIRATIONS, IDREIS AND JOHARI. ALWAYS BE THE BEST YOU CAN BE AND ROCK DOING IT!

CONTRIBUTORS AND SUPPORTERS

ADVISOR	JOHARI SHERMAN
ULTIMATE CREATOR	SHARON SPENCE
WONDER WOMAN	TRINA WILLIAMS
BIGGEST FAN	LYNN HICKS
CREATIVE TWIN	DESTINI HINKLE
SOUTHERN BELLE	TRACEY DOBBINS
BELIZEAN BEAUTY	KARYL HUGHLETT
POSITIVE PATTI	RASHADA WHITEHEAD

SEE OUR OTHER PRODUCTS ONLINE:
WWW.KEE2CREATIVITY.COM
KEE@KEE2CREATIVITY.COM

EDITOR'S NOTE

There is something unmistakably cool about a woman who's completely at ease in her clothes -- and in her own skin. The key to scoring that elusive confidence? That's where we come in. Penelope Girly is all about helping you find your inner cover girl, the passion that lies within, that cozy headspace where you stand a little taller, smile a bit brighter, and a simply stop second-guessing yourself. Whether you're a fashionista or a sophisticate, enjoy your own perfectly executed magazine that's all about you! Grace the blank pages with positive notes, add your input to the headlines, make it your own and let your cover girl come to life. So turn the page and dive right in!

Penelope GIRLY

Being yourself **NEVER** *goes out of style!*

" **YOU CAN LIKE NORMAL, I'M GOING TO LIKE WHAT'S ME.
-ARKEELAUS D. SHERMAN** "

PENELOPE GIRLY | VOL. 1 ISSUE 1   KEE2CREATIVITY
                                      COPYRIGHT © 2011-2012

be you!

be bold
be kind
be loving
be beautiful
be fabulous
be positive
be strong
be humble
be patient
be honest
be intelligent
be ambitious
be focused
be intriguing
be open minded
be self-assured
be compassionate
be goal-oriented
be mindful of others
be aware of your surroundings

PENELOPE GIRLY | VOL. 1 ISSUE 1   KEE2CREATIVITY
                                                   COPYRIGHT © 2011-2012

Haute List!
See it. Own it. Love it.

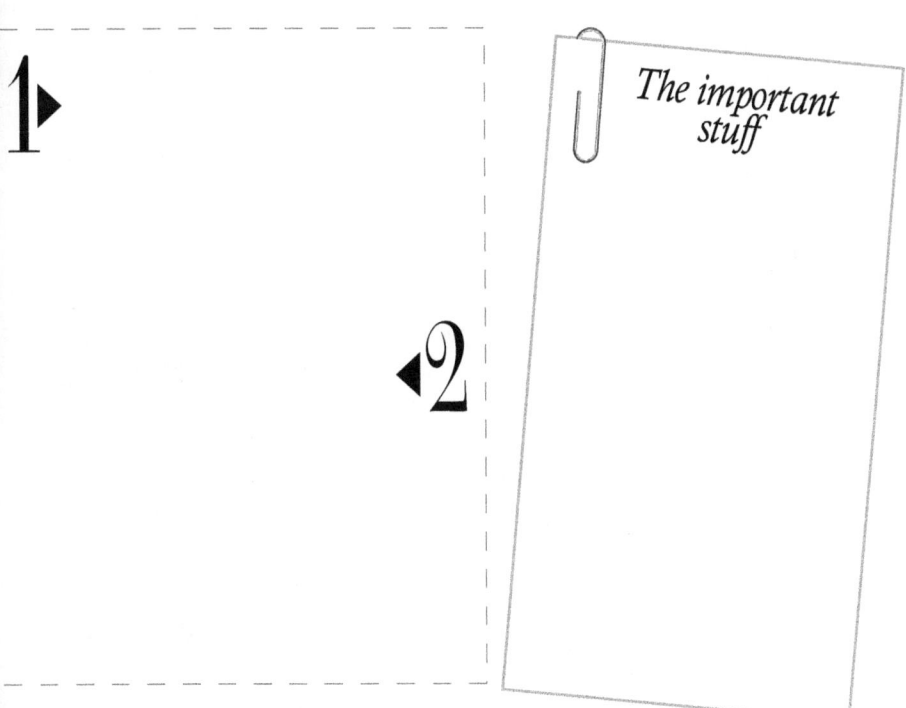

1▶

◀2 The important stuff

[3▶

5▶

4▶]

PENELOPE GIRLY | VOL. 1 ISSUE 1   KEE2CREATIVITY
                                        COPYRIGHT © 2011-2012

find
beauty
within

———— **LUXE** *is a must* ————

LUXE *is a must*

PENELOPE GIRLY | VOL. 1 ISSUE 1   KEE2CREATIVITY
                                        COPYRIGHT © 2011-2012

PENELOPE GIRLY | VOL. 1 ISSUE 1 KEE2CREATIVITY
COPYRIGHT © 2011-2012

I'm **EVERY** *woman*

I'm **EVERY** *woman*

EVERY fashionista BREAKS THE RULES

STAND **OUT** FROM THE CROWD!

PENELOPE GIRLY | VOL. 1 ISSUE 1   KEE2CREATIVITY
                                                    COPYRIGHT © 2011-2012

PENELOPE GIRLY | VOL. 1 ISSUE 1   KEE2CREATIVITY
COPYRIGHT © 2011-2012

more BRIGHT IDEAS

and brighter ones!

PENELOPE GIRLY | VOL. 1 ISSUE 1   KEE2CREATIVITY
COPYRIGHT © 2011-2012

PENELOPE GIRLY | VOL. 1 ISSUE 1   KEE2CREATIVITY
COPYRIGHT © 2011-2012

what works for me

BEAUTY | OBSESSIONS

Fab Beauty Finds:
Priceless

EYE CANDY
Captivate with eye contact, it's easy to apply and ideal for displaying confidence.

POLISH
Paint a positive outlook and enjoy a no-mess day with just a few strokes.

TWEEZE
pluck away all negative thoughts, people and influences, creating a perfect arch towards fabulous-ity!

GLOW
Marvel your audience with life and enthusiasm; let your smile set things in motion.

PENELOPE GIRLY | VOL. 1 ISSUE 1

KEE2CREATIVITY
COPYRIGHT © 2011-2012

PENELOPE GIRLY | VOL. 1 ISSUE 1

KEE2CREATIVITY
COPYRIGHT © 2011-2012

Haute List!
See it. Own it. Love it.

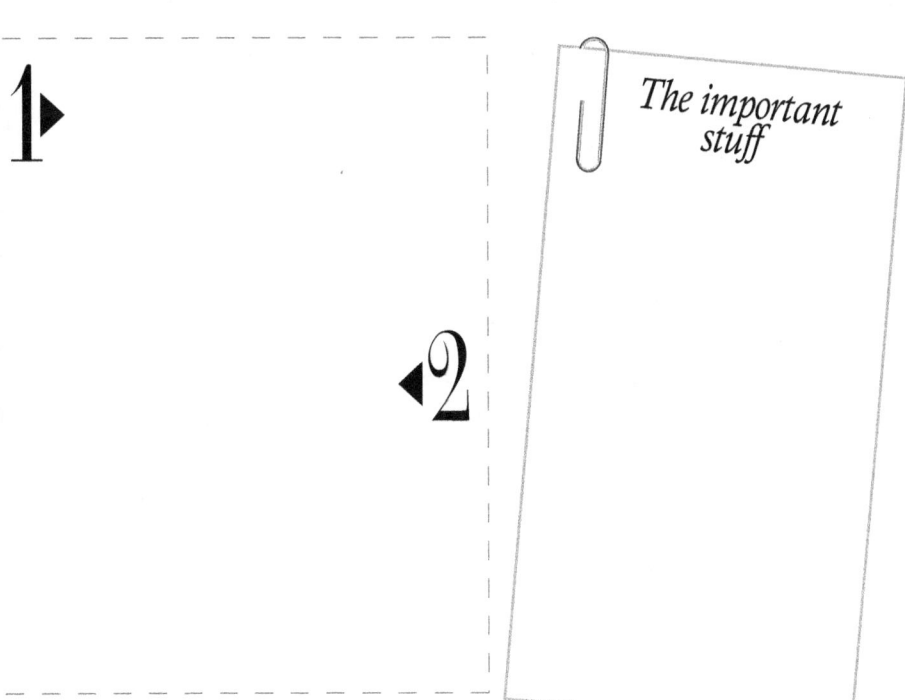

The important stuff

1▶

◀2

[3▶

5▶

4▶]

The cover girl of our latest issue tells us what she can't live wihout!

beloved
book...

{ *dreaming of..* }

CAN'T GET ENOUGH OF...

FASHION OBSESSIONS...

HAPPY I BOUGHT...

MY GUILTY PLEASURE...

vital BEAUTY PRODUCTS...

TOP SHOPS

WHEN I LEAVE MY HOUSE I TAKE....

PENELOPE GIRLY | VOL. 1 ISSUE 1

KEE2CREATIVITY
COPYRIGHT © 2011-2012

THE craveLIST

We want them, We need them!
8 Things you can't live without!

1.

2.

3.

4.

5.

6.

7.

8.

PENELOPE GIRLY | VOL. 1 ISSUE 1
KEE2CREATIVITY
COPYRIGHT © 2011-2012

PENELOPE GIRLY | VOL. 1 ISSUE 1   KEE2CREATIVITY
COPYRIGHT © 2011-2012

PENELOPE GIRLY | VOL. 1 ISSUE 1   KEE2CREATIVITY
                                              COPYRIGHT © 2011-2012

TIMELESS TRENDS

{EMBELLISHED}
Add a bit of sparkle, subtle shine has a greater impact than outright color. Pretend its no big deal, naturally have your attitude reflect and refract light!

TIMELESS TRENDS

{SAFARI}

This season's forecast highlights dreams that aren't truly out of your compass. The mood is adventurous, as you journey into the wild of achievable. Pair these strong elements with research and ambitious and you're on the tour of your life.

TIMELESS TRENDS

{HOURGLASS}

Always celebrate your curves! Embrace, even enhance, the shape you're in. Define your waist creating two dramatic set of curves to proclaim your femininity. Find which proportion flatters you; and also dress according to your body type.

TIMELESS TRENDS

{SILKY}

This kinder, gentler variation is an easy way to be. Its soft and airy palette offers risk free simplicity in a soft and pretty mood. Step into a softer side of you, no need to over accessorize.

PENELOPE GIRLY | VOL. 1 ISSUE 1

KEE2CREATIVITY
COPYRIGHT © 2011-2012

PENELOPE GIRLY | VOL. 1 ISSUE 1 KEE2CREATIVITY
COPYRIGHT © 2011-2012

PENELOPE GIRLY | VOL. 1 ISSUE 1 KEE2CREATIVITY
COPYRIGHT © 2011-2012

PENELOPE GIRLY | VOL. 1 ISSUE 1   KEE2CREATIVITY
COPYRIGHT © 2011-2012

PENELOPE GIRLY | VOL. 1 ISSUE 1   KEE2CREATIVITY
                                        COPYRIGHT © 2011-2012

PENELOPE GIRLY | VOL. 1 ISSUE 1

KEE2CREATIVITY
COPYRIGHT © 2011-2012

Haute List!
See it. Own it. Love it.

1▶

◀2

The important stuff

[3▶

5▶

4▶

PENELOPE GIRLY | VOL. 1 ISSUE 1

KEE2CREATIVITY
COPYRIGHT © 2011-2012

PENELOPE GIRLY | VOL. 1 ISSUE 1   KEE2CREATIVITY
                                                               COPYRIGHT © 2011-2012

PENELOPE GIRLY | VOL. 1 ISSUE 1   KEE2CREATIVITY
                                                    COPYRIGHT © 2011-2012

HOW TO BE Armed & fabulous

THE TOP TEN
best tips of all time!

BE FABULOUS, CONFIDENT AND ARMED WITH TOOLS THAT PULL IT ALL TOGETHER WITH PANACHE!

1. *Flaunt brains* THEN *beauty*

EMBRACE *your shape* 2.

4. THINK
before speaking

3. ADD
a touch of class

5. OPEN *your mind*

ACCENTUATE *your positive* 6.

7. CONQUER *your fears*

8. STAY *humble*

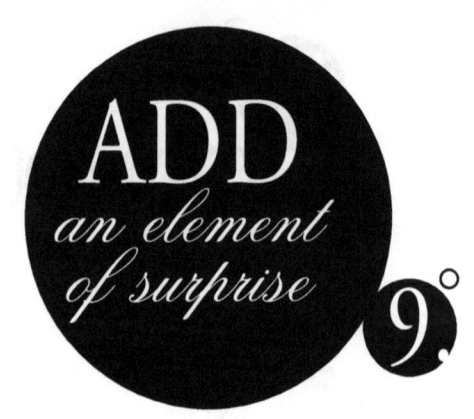

PENELOPE GIRLY | VOL. 1 ISSUE 1   KEE2CREATIVITY
COPYRIGHT © 2011-2012

PENELOPE GIRLY | VOL. 1 ISSUE 1   KEE2CREATIVITY
COPYRIGHT © 2011-2012

ah hah MOMENT....

PENELOPE GIRLY | VOL. 1 ISSUE 1   KEE2CREATIVITY
COPYRIGHT © 2011-2012

PENELOPE GIRLY | VOL. 1 ISSUE 1

KEE2CREATIVITY
COPYRIGHT © 2011-2012

PENELOPE GIRLY | VOL. 1 ISSUE 1   KEE2CREATIVITY
COPYRIGHT © 2011-2012

PENELOPE GIRLY | VOL. 1 ISSUE 1 KEE2CREATIVITY
COPYRIGHT © 2011-2012

PENELOPE GIRLY | VOL. 1 ISSUE 1   KEE2CREATIVITY
COPYRIGHT © 2011-2012

PENELOPE GIRLY | VOL. 1 ISSUE 1 KEE2CREATIVITY
COPYRIGHT © 2011-2012

all about the details!

PENELOPE GIRLY | VOL. 1 ISSUE 1

KEE2CREATIVITY
COPYRIGHT © 2011-2012

PENELOPE GIRLY | VOL. 1 ISSUE 1

KEE2CREATIVITY
COPYRIGHT © 2011-2012

PENELOPE GIRLY | VOL. 1 ISSUE 1   KEE2CREATIVITY
                                                    COPYRIGHT © 2011-2012

PENELOPE GIRLY | VOL. 1 ISSUE 1

KEE2CREATIVITY
COPYRIGHT © 2011-2012

SAME PASSION DIFFERENT DIRECTION

All the excitement to bring your passions out!

Passion Forward is all about being true to yourself, being fearless in declaring the depths of your integrity, imagination and capturing the essence of your spirit in a tangible act of outward expressions.

ALL-NEW FOCUS.

DISCOVER YOUR PASSION

A passion is a compelling or strong emotion towards something you love! WHAT ARE YOU PASSIONATE ABOUT?

BE FEARLESS

It's a difficult undertaking, as it takes a sense of adventure, some of your ideas may be a success, as other will fail. When making steps towards living your passion , don't get scared! WHAT ARE YOUR CHALLENGES? WHAT IS YOUR PLAN TO OVERCOME THEM?

PERSONALIZE YOUR PASSION

If you want to stay ahead of the trends, be the one setting them instead of following them. If you want to turn your passion into action, put your personal spin on things to stand out! WHAT IS YOUR SPIN ON THINGS?

IDEAS

JOT DOWN YOUR IDEAS ON YOUR JOURNEY TOWARDS BEING PASSION FORWARD!

RESEARCH »

RESEARCH! RESEARCH! RESEARCH! IT'S ALWAYS NEEDED WHEN TURNING YOUR PASSION INTO ACTION!

ACTION »

Now is the time to set your plan into action. Being Passion Forward takes risk, move forward and follow your heart!
JOT DOWN YOUR PLAN!

www.ingramcontent.com/pod-product-compliance
Lightning Source LLC
Chambersburg PA
CBHW060837050426
42453CB00008B/732